WISCONSIN POST OFFICE MURAL GUIDEBOOK

DAVID W. GATES JR.

POST OFFICE FANS

Crystal Lake, Illinois

Post Office Fans
PO Box 11
Crystal Lake, IL 60039
Phone: 815-206-8405
info@postofficefans.com • www.postofficefans.com

Cover and text design by John Reinhardt Book Design
Front cover photo: Chilton Post Office, Chilton, Wisconsin

CONTENTS

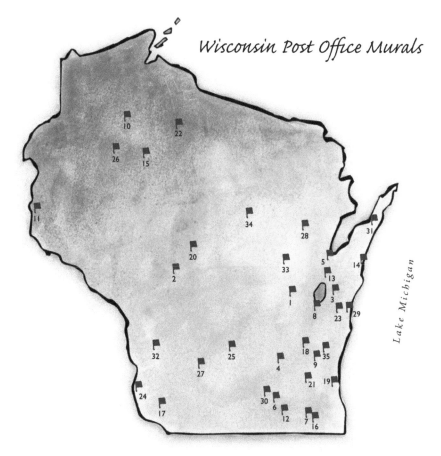

Wisconsin Post Office Murals

PREFACE

THE STATISTICS I'VE READ report there are somewhere between 1,100 and 1,400 works of art located in public post offices nationwide. Since I've been unable to verify these statistics, I've made it my mission to find out exactly how many exist and view them all.

What began for me as a casual interest in a photographic subject soon became a deep fascination with the history and presence of a unique moment in American culture and art. Before creating this guidebook, I visited hundreds of post offices and spoke to dozens of people across the U.S.—we were united in our enthusiasm for keeping the stories of this art alive and available for the American public.

The guidebook you are viewing today is an account of all 35 of Wisconsin's New Deal post office murals. I encourage you to visit one of these post offices in Wisconsin or seek out one in your own state. To learn about this special art is to learn about the continuing American journey.

This is the reference I wish I had when I started this project. When I visited my first post office with a mural, I never found a complete list or status of all the murals in Wisconsin. I had to research each one individually, then drive out to photograph it. As my interest grew, I wanted something I could use as a quick reference for all the locations in Wisconsin. This led to the guidebook you are holding today. It provides a quick reference to the New Deal murals in Wisconsin.

I've created this guidebook for your benefit, in case you find yourself needing the same checklist as you travel and discover each building and mural. I hope this book brings you enjoyment and knowledge. There is no need to scour multiple sources to find each one. I've done the work for you. Print it out or download it to your mobile device to bring with you on your next post office visit.

Thank you,

David W. Gates Jr.

INTRODUCTION

FROM 1934–1943, fascinating murals and various forms of art were commissioned and installed in public buildings under the United States Treasury Department's Section of Painting and Sculpture, later renamed the Section of Fine Arts.

My research revealed two reasons for installing art in post offices; the first was to bring light and hope to a country gripped by the Great Depression, and the second was to employ artists during this difficult time.

Anonymous competitions were held to select artists for new federal buildings that were being constructed during this time. Commissions paid to the artists were approximately one percent of the congressional appropriation to construct the new post office building.

This informative book lists all the post offices in Wisconsin that received artwork. It gives you a quick reference to the New Deal post office murals in Wisconsin. It includes:

- Full address
- Artist
- Title
- Medium
- Status
- Link for further reading

I make no distinctions about the media used for each piece of artwork. If the art is a painting on the wall, I refer to it as a mural. There is no distinction between oil on canvas, fresco, or egg tempera. I simply want to alert the reader what to look for when visiting the post office.

Not all buildings have murals; other mediums were used such as wood, plaster, metal, or stone.

BERLIN

ADDRESS: 122 S. Pearl St., Berlin, Wisconsin 54923

ARTIST: Raymond Redell

TITLE: *Gathering Cranberries*

MEDIUM: Mural

STATUS: The Berlin post office is still an active, operating facility, and the mural can be viewed by interested members of the public. It resides in the lobby on the wall above the postmaster's door.

WEB: www.postofficefans.com/berlin-wisconsin-post-office/

Black River Falls

ADDRESS: 108 Filmore St., Black River Falls, Wisconsin 54615

ARTIST: Frank Buffmire

TITLE: *Lumbering Black River Mill*

MEDIUM: Mural

STATUS: The Black River Falls Post Office is active to this day, and the mural is viewable by the public. It resides in the lobby on the wall above the postmaster's door.

WEB: www.postofficefans.com/black-river-falls-wisconsin-post-office/

CHILTON

ADDRESS: 57 E. Main St., Chilton, Wisconsin 53014

ARTIST: Charles W. Thwaites

TITLE: *Threshing Barley*

MEDIUM: Mural

STATUS: The Chilton Post Office is active to this day, and the mural is accessible to members of the public. It resides in the lobby on the wall above the postmaster's door.

WEB: www.postofficefans.com/chilton-wisconsin-post-office/

COLUMBUS

ADDRESS: 211 S. Dickason Blvd., Columbus, Wisconsin 53925

ARTIST: Arnold Blanch

TITLE: *One Hundredth Anniversary*

MEDIUM: Mural

STATUS: This is still an active post office, and the mural can be viewed by the public. It resides in the lobby on the wall above the postmaster's door.

WEB: www.postofficefans.com/columbus-wisconsin-post-office/

DE PERE

ADDRESS: 416 George St., De Pere, Wisconsin 54115

ARTIST: Lester W. Bentley

TITLE: *The Red Pieta, Nicholas Perot, and Give Us This Day*

MEDIUM: Three individual mural panels.

STATUS: The murals no longer reside in the original building on George Street. They have been moved to the Neville Public Museum in Green Bay, Wisconsin.

Call ahead to verify the hours of the museum before heading out to view this one. The panels were located on the wall of one of the stairwells of the museum.

WEB: www.postofficefans.com/former-de-pere-wisconsin-post-office/

EDGERTON

ADDRESS: 104 Swift St., Edgerton, Wisconsin 53534

ARTIST: Vladimir Rousseff

TITLE: *Tobacco Harvest*

MEDIUM: Mural

STATUS: The Edgerton Post Office exists to this day, and the mural is still accessible to members of the public interested in viewing it. It resides in the lobby on the wall above the postmaster's door.

WEB: www.postofficefans.com/edgerton-wisconsin-post-office/

ELKHORN

ADDRESS: 102 E. Walworth St., Elkhorn, Wisconsin 53121

ARTIST: Tom Rost

TITLE: *Pioneer Postman*

MEDIUM: Mural

STATUS: The Elkhorn Post Office is still active up to this day and the mural viewable by members of the public. It resides in the lobby on the wall above the postmaster's door.

WEB: www.postofficefans.com/elkhorn-wisconsin-post-office/

FOND DU LAC

ADDRESS: 19 E. 1st St., Fond du Lac, Wisconsin 54935

ARTIST: Boris Gilbertson

TITLE: *Birds and Animals of the Northwest*

MEDIUM: Limestone reliefs

STATUS: The original building is no longer the post office. The 11 limestone reliefs are on the exterior of the building and can be observed by interested parties.

WEB: www.postofficefans.com/former-fond-du-lac-wisconsin-post-office/

HARTFORD

ADDRESS: 35 E. Sumner St., Hartford, Wisconsin 53027

ARTIST: Ethel Spears

TITLE: *Autumn Wisconsin Landscapes*

MEDIUM: Mural

STATUS: The mural has been transferred to the Schauer Arts Center and is only viewable during business hours.

If visiting the Schauer Center, be sure to call ahead and verify the hours.

WEB: www.postofficefans.com/former-hartford-wisconsin-post-office/

HAYWARD

ADDRESS: 10597 Main St., Hayward, Wisconsin 54843

ARTIST: Stella E. Harlos

TITLE: *The Land of Woods and Lakes*

MEDIUM: Mural

STATUS: This mural still exists in the Hayward Post Office and can be viewed by interested members of the public. It resides in the lobby on the wall above the postmaster's door.

WEB: www.postofficefans.com/hayward-wisconsin-post-office/

HUDSON

ADDRESS: 225 Locust St., Hudson, Wisconsin 54016

ARTIST: Ruth Grotenrath

TITLE: *Unloading a River Barge*

MEDIUM: Mural

STATUS: The mural no longer resides in the original Hudson Post Office building. It was moved to the Museum of Wisconsin ARTISTS (MOWA) located in West Bend, Wisconsin. At the time of writing, the mural was in storage and not available for viewing by the public.

WEB: www.postofficefans.com/former-hudson-wisconsin-post-office/

JANESVILLE

ADDRESS: 210 Dodge St., Janesville, Wisconsin 53545

ARTIST: Boris Gilbertson

TITLE: *Wild Ducks*

MEDIUM: Aluminum Panels

STATUS: The aluminum panels made for Janesville by Gilbertson are now in the newer post office where they are only available for viewing during business hours. The lobby has a locked retail section where the panels are located.

WEB: www.postofficefans.com/former-janesville-wisconsin-post-office/

KAUKAUNA

ADDRESS: 112 Main St., Kaukauna, Wisconsin 54130

ARTIST: Vladimir Rousseff

TITLE: *A. Grignon Trading with the Indians*

MEDIUM: Mural

STATUS: The mural no longer resides in the original building and has since been moved to the new post office building located on Dotty Street. The mural is in the main lobby.

WEB: www.postofficefans.com/kaukauna-wisconsin-post-office/

KEWAUNEE

ADDRESS: 119 Ellis St., Kewaunee, Wisconsin 54216

ARTIST: Paul Faulkner

TITLE: *Winter Sports*

MEDIUM: Mural

STATUS: The Kewaunee Post Office is still active and the mural is still accessible to members of the public interested in viewing it. It resides in the lobby on the wall above the postmaster's door.

WEB: www.postofficefans.com/kewaunee-wisconsin-post-office/

LADYSMITH

ADDRESS: 212 Miner Ave., Ladysmith, Wisconsin 54848

ARTIST: Elsa Jemne

TITLE: *Development of the Land*

MEDIUM: Mural

STATUS: The mural is no longer viewable, having either been destroyed or painted over. None of my research has confirmed the fate of this artwork. There is an original black and white photograph on file at the National Archives, College Park Maryland for viewing.

WEB: www.postofficefans.com/ladysmith-wisconsin-post-office/

LAKE GENEVA

ADDRESS: 672 W. Main St., Lake Geneva, Wisconsin 53147

ARTIST: George A. Dietrich

TITLE: *Winter Landscapes*

MEDIUM: Mural

STATUS: The mural is still present in the post office. It is accessible to members of the public interested in viewing it. It resides in the lobby on the wall above the postmaster's door.

WEB: www.postofficefans.com/lake-geneva-wisconsin-post-office/

LANCASTER

ADDRESS: 236 W. Main St., Lancaster, Wisconsin 53813

ARTIST: Tom Rost

TITLE: *Farm Yard*

MEDIUM: Mural

STATUS: The Lancaster Post Office is still active and the mural accessible to the public. It resides in the lobby on the wall above the post-master's door.

WEB: www.postofficefans.com/lancaster-wisconsin-post-office/

MAYVILLE

ADDRESS: 7 N. School St., Mayville, Wisconsin 53050

ARTIST: Peter Rotier

TITLE: *Wisconsin Rural Scene*

MEDIUM: Mural

STATUS: This post office is still active and the mural viewable by interested members of the public. It resides in the lobby on the wall above the postmaster's door.

WEB: www.postofficefans.com/mayville-wisconsin-post-office/

MILWAUKEE

ADDRESS: 7440 W. Greenfield Ave., Milwaukee, Wisconsin 53214

ARTIST: Frances Foy

TITLE: *Wisconsin Wildflowers—Spring, Wisconsin Wildflowers–Autumn*

MEDIUM: Murals

STATUS: The West Allis Branch Post Office is still active and the two murals are viewable. One resides on the wall above the postmaster's door. The other is on the opposite side of the lobby.

WEB: www.postofficefans.com/milwaukee-west-allis-wisconsin-post-office/

NEILLSVILLE

ADDRESS: 619 Hewett St., Neillsville, Wisconsin 54456

ARTIST: John Van Koert

TITLE: *The Choosing of the County Seat*

MEDIUM: Mural

STATUS: The Neillsville Post Office is still active and the mural is viewable by the public. It resides in the lobby on the wall above the postmaster's door.

WEB: www.postofficefans.com/neillsville-wisconsin-post-office/

Oconomowoc

ADDRESS: 38 S. Main St., Oconomowoc, Wisconsin 53066

ARTIST: Edward Morton

TITLE: *Winter Sports and Rabbit Hunters*

MEDIUM: Mural

STATUS: The Oconomowoc Post Office is still active and the mural viewable by the public. It resides on the wall of the main lobby.

WEB: www.postofficefans.com/oconomowoc-wisconsin-post-office/

PARK FALLS

ADDRESS: 109 1st St., Park Falls, Wisconsin 54552

ARTIST: James S. Waltrous

TITLE: *Lumberjack Fight on the Flambeau River*

MEDIUM: Mural

STATUS: The Park Falls Post Office is still active and the mural decoration remains viewable by the public. It resides in the lobby on the wall above the postmaster's door.

WEB: www.postofficefans.com/park-falls-wisconsin-post-office/

PLYMOUTH

ADDRESS: 302 E. Main St., Plymouth, Wisconsin 53073

ARTIST: Charles W. Thwaites

TITLE: *Making Cheese*

MEDIUM: Mural

STATUS: The Plymouth Post Office is still active and the mural painting viewable by the public. It resides in the lobby on the wall above the postmaster's door.

WEB: www.postofficefans.com/plymouth-wisconsin-post-office/

PRAIRIE DU CHIEN

ADDRESS: 120 S. Beaumont Rd., Prairie du Chien, Wisconsin 53821

ARTIST: Jefferson E. Greer

TITLE: *Discovery of Northern Waters of the Mississippi*

MEDIUM: Plaster cast

STATUS: Prairie du Chien is still an active post office and the plaster cast is available for viewing. It resides in the lobby on the wall above the postmaster's door.

WEB: www.postofficefans.com/prairie-du-chien-wisconsin-post-office/

REEDSBURG

ADDRESS: 215 N. Walnut St., Reedsburg, Wisconsin 53959

ARTIST: Richard Jansen

TITLE: *Dairy Farming*

MEDIUM: Mural

STATUS: The Reedsburg post office is still active, and the mural is viewable by the public. It resides in the lobby on the wall above the postmaster's door.

WEB: www.postofficefans.com/reedsburg-wisconsin-post-office/

RICE LAKE

ADDRESS: 14 E. Eau Claire St., Rice Lake, Wisconsin 54868

ARTIST: Forrest Flower

TITLE: *Rural Delivery*

MEDIUM: Mural

STATUS: The Rice Lake Post Office is still active and the mural is viewable by the public. It resides in the lobby on the wall above the postmaster's door.

WEB: www.postofficefans.com/rice-lake-wisconsin-post-office/

RICHLAND CENTER

ADDRESS: 213 N. Central Ave., Richland Center, Wisconsin 53581

ARTIST: Richard Brooks

TITLE: *Decorative Interpretation of Unification of America through the Post*

MEDIUM: Mural

STATUS: The Richland Center Post Office is still active and the mural viewable by the public. It resides in the lobby on the wall above the postmaster's door.

WEB: www.postofficefans.com/richland-center-wisconsin-post-office/

Shawano

ADDRESS: 235 S. Main St., Shawano, Wisconsin 54166

ARTIST: Eugene Higgins

TITLE: *The First Settlers*

MEDIUM: Mural

STATUS: The Post Office in Shawano is still active and the mural is view-able by the public. It resides in the lobby on the wall above the postmaster's door.

WEB: www.postofficefans.com/shawano-wisconsin-post-office/

SHEBOYGAN

ADDRESS: 522 N. 9th St., Sheboygan, Wisconsin 53081

ARTIST: Schomer Lichtner

TITLE: *Agriculture, Indian Life, Present City, The Lake, The Pioneer*

MEDIUM: Murals

STATUS: The Sheboygan Post Office is still active and all the murals are viewable by the public. They reside on the walls in the main lobby.

WEB: www.postofficefans.com/sheboygan-wisconsin-post-office/

STOUGHTON

ADDRESS: 246 E. Main St., Stoughton, Wisconsin 53589

ARTIST: Edmund D. Lewandowski

TITLE: *Air Mail Service*

MEDIUM: Mural

STATUS: The Stoughton Post Office is still active and the mural viewable by the public. It resides in the lobby on the wall above the post-master's door.

WEB: www.postofficefans.com/stoughton-wisconsin-post-office/

STURGEON BAY

ADDRESS: 359 Louisiana, Sturgeon Bay, Wisconsin 54235

ARTIST: Santos Zingale

TITLE: *Fruits of Sturgeon Bay*

MEDIUM: Mural

STATUS: The Sturgeon Bay Post Office is still active and the mural view-able by the public. It resides in the lobby on the wall above the postmaster's door.

WEB: www.postofficefans.com/sturgeon-bay-wisconsin-post-office/

VIROQUA

ADDRESS: 119 E. Jefferson St., Viroqua, Wisconsin 54665

ARTIST: Forrest Flower

TITLE: *War Party*

MEDIUM: Mural

STATUS: The Viroqua Post Office is still active and the mural viewable. It resides in the lobby on the wall above the postmaster's door.

WEB: www.postofficefans.com/viroqua-wisconsin-post-office/

WAUPACA

ADDRESS: 306 S. Main St., Waupaca, Wisconsin 54981

ARTIST: Raymond Redell

TITLE: *Wisconsin Countryside*

MEDIUM: Mural

STATUS: The Waupaca Post Office is still active and the mural viewable by the public. It resides in the lobby on the wall above the post-master's door.

WEB: www.postofficefans.com/waupaca-wisconsin-post-office/

WAUSAU

ADDRESS: 317 1st St., Wausau, Wisconsin 54403

ARTIST: Gerrit Sinclair

TITLE: *Lumbering, Rural Mail*

MEDIUM: Murals

STATUS: Unfortunately, the post office building was sold and converted to apartments. Lumbering still resides in the main lobby. Since the building is locked and only accessible to residents, it is no longer accessible to members of the public.

The STATUS or whereabouts of the second mural *Rural Mail* remain a mystery to this day. If you have any information in regards to this one, we'd love to hear from you. Please contact us.

If heading to Wausau, you could contact the management office to request access to the mural.

WEB: www.postofficefans.com/former-wausau-wisconsin-post-office/

WEST BEND

ADDRESS: 607 Elm St., West Bend, Wisconsin 53095

ARTIST: Peter Rotier

TITLE: *The Rural Mail Carrier*

MEDIUM: Mural

STATUS: The West Bend Post Office is still active and the mural viewable by the public. It resides in the lobby on the wall above the postmaster's door.

WEB: www.postofficefans.com/west-bend-wisconsin-post-office/

SUMMARY

I CREATED THIS BOOK as a reference for myself, as well as for those who are interested in these wonderful buildings and works of art. My goal is to provide you a valuable reference list of the buildings in Wisconsin that house murals. For more information about each one and to participate in the discussion of any of the buildings or art, please visit www.postofficefans.com.

This book contains all the post offices in Wisconsin that had art installed as a part of the New Deal. This book provides notes on the location and accessibility of the art. I've personally visited and photographed each building. Please note this is not a complete list of all the post office buildings constructed in Wisconsin during the New Deal, only the ones that housed art.

I welcome your comments, suggestions, or feedback. You may reach me through the following social channels. Of course, I also welcome mail through the United States Postal Service.

ABOUT THE AUTHOR

DAVID W. GATES JR. is a post office enthusiast who has traveled thousands of miles nationwide in search of historic post office buildings and art.

He blogs about his work at:

www.postofficefans.com

Although the murals have been around for more than 85 years, David discovered how often these are overlooked. Join David in his quest to visit them all.

He lives in Crystal Lake, IL with his wife, son and two cats. When not photographing and documenting post offices, he can be found cooking, baking, hiking, or involved in do-it- yourself projects at home, not necessarily all at once and not necessarily in that order.

WISCONSIN POST OFFICE MURALS

by David W. Gates Jr.

Wisconsin Post Office Murals dives deeper into the particulars, including how the murals were developed by the ARTISTS. The correspondence and letters created during this time provide an fascinating glimpse of our nation's history. The author's research reveals the efforts of the government and local communities during this time. Not every community was thrilled with the idea of the subject matter or money spent on artwork for their local post office building.

The murals were installed in small communities throughout Wisconsin on purpose. They were meant to bring significant art to everyday Americans. This is public art and the post office was the most public of places during this era. One hundred sixty full color images celebrate these wonderful pieces of art as they exist today. Seventy color images of the buildings give the reader a sense of being there. **Wisconsin Post Office Murals** is the arm-chair traveler's guide to post office murals in Wisconsin.

If you have enjoyed this book or found it useful,
please share it with your family, friends,
and social media followers.

CPSIA information can be obtained
at www.ICGtesting.com
Printed in the USA
BVHW020322160319
542847BV00007B/70/P

9 781970 088090